VIDEO BOOK

JAKE SHIMABUK...es
UKULELE LESSONS

Learn Notes, Chords, Songs, and Playing Techniques from the Master of Modern Ukulele

To access video visit:
www.halleonard.com/mylibrary

Enter Code
2324-9874-4854-0788

Video directed by Coleman Saunders
Cover photo: Coleman Saunders

ISBN 978-1-4950-6285-8

7777 W. BLUEMOUND RD. P.O. BOX 13819 MILWAUKEE, WI 53213

In Australia Contact:
Hal Leonard Australia Pty. Ltd.
4 Lentara Court
Cheltenham, Victoria, 3192 Australia
Email: ausadmin@halleonard.com.au

Visit Hal Leonard Online at
www.halleonard.com

CONTENTS

VIDEO LESSONS

BONUS SONG TRANSCRIPTIONS
OF LIVE VIDEO PERFORMANCES

INTRODUCTION

Over ten years ago, while I was waiting for my bags at JFK airport, a man walked up to me and said, "What's in the case?" I replied, "It's an ukulele." Then he laughed and said, "You play the *yuu-kuu-lay-lee*? Good luck with that."

In Hawaii, the ukulele is a well-respected instrument and an important part of Hawaiian culture. I'm never offended, though, when people don't take the instrument seriously because I don't think any instrument should be taken too seriously. The beautiful thing about the ukulele is that it's not intimidating. If you told someone who has never played an instrument before to start playing the violin, piano, or guitar, they would immediately cringe and say, "That's too hard," or "I don't have any musical talent." But if you mention the ukulele, they'll usually say, "Sure, that sounds like fun!"

Music is not just the universal language, it is the language of the universe. It's the language of human emotion. Whether we know it or not, we are all musicians because we feel things like joy, anger, sadness, fear, etc. Music is simply the verbal or audio expression of these feelings.

I hope that this video and accompanying book will serve as a friendly introduction to music as well as this wonderful four-string Hawaiian instrument. The ukulele has brought me so much over the years and I hope it will do the same for you.

So take it slow, have fun and share your music with the rest of the world!

Jake

ABOUT THE VIDEO

Each video lesson includes a chapter in the book with written examples, so you can see and hear the material being taught. To access all of the videos that accompany this book, simply go to **www.halleonard.com/mylibrary** and enter the code found on page 1. The music examples within the book are marked with an icon and timecode to tell you exactly where on the video the example is performed.

CHAPTER 1
GETTING STARTED

The example below shows the notes of the open strings on the ukulele.

Ukulele music is written with notes on a **staff**, and also in **tablature** (tab). The note staff has five lines and four spaces between the lines. Where a note is written on this staff determines its pitch. Reading music on the note staff is not necessary to play the lessons in this book, but is included for users who already read and may like to have both.

Located just below the note staff, tablature consists of four horizontal lines that represent the strings of the instrument. These strings are also referred to as "floors" through the video. The numbers on the lines indicate which fret, or "stall," to play on that string (0 = open). Tab makes it possible for anyone to read a piece of music without having to learn all the notes of the normal music staff first.

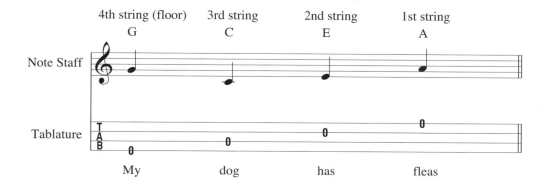

Tuning: 5–4–2 Method

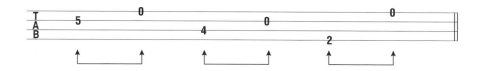

- First, tune your 1st string using an electronic tuner, tuning fork, or other reference pitch.
- Then play the 5th fret of your 2nd string and tune that pitch to match the open 1st string.
- Next, play the 4th fret of the 3rd string, and tune that pitch to your open 2nd string.
- Finally, play the 2nd fret of the 4th string and match that pitch to your open 1st string.

Twinkle, Twinkle Little Star

(8:20)

CHAPTER 2
FRETTING NOTES

Hot Cross Buns - 1st Floor

(4:20)

Traditional
Copyright © 2017 by HAL LEONARD LLC
International Copyright Secured   All Rights Reserved

Mary Had a Little Lamb

(4:54)

Words by Sarah Josepha Hale
Traditional Music
Copyright © 2017 by HAL LEONARD LLC
International Copyright Secured   All Rights Reserved

Hot Cross Buns - 2nd Floor

(5:20)

Traditional
Copyright © 2017 by HAL LEONARD LLC
International Copyright Secured   All Rights Reserved

Hot Cross Buns - 3rd Floor

(6:00)

Traditional
Copyright © 2017 by HAL LEONARD LLC
International Copyright Secured   All Rights Reserved

Hot Cross Buns - 4th Floor

(6:14)

Twinkle, Twinkle Little Star

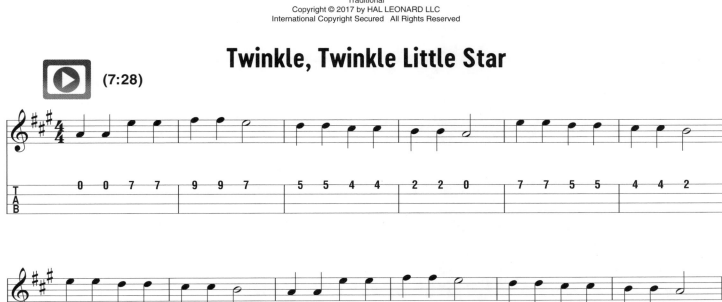

(7:28)

Happy Birthday to You - 1st Floor

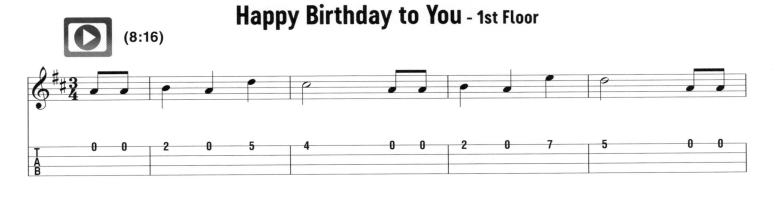

(8:16)

Happy Birthday to You - 2nd Floor

(9:04)

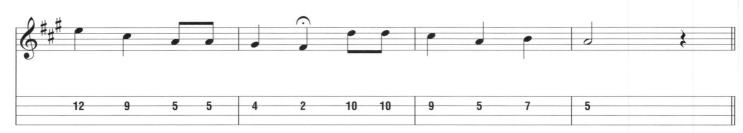

To perform "Happy Birthday to You" on the 3rd floor, simply play the same tab numbers you just did on floors 1 and 2, but on the 3rd string.

The Star Spangled Banner

(10:26)

Moderately slow

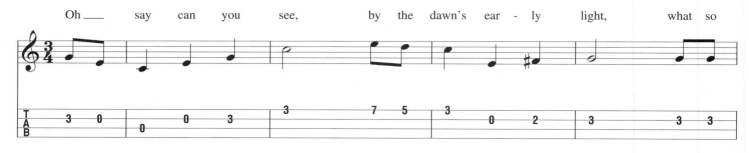

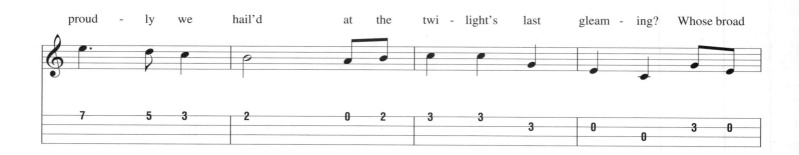

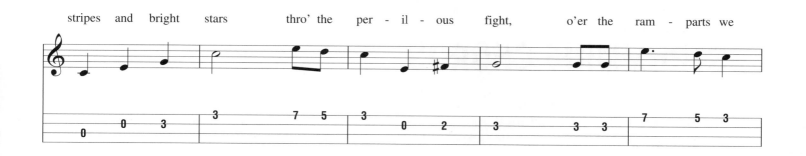

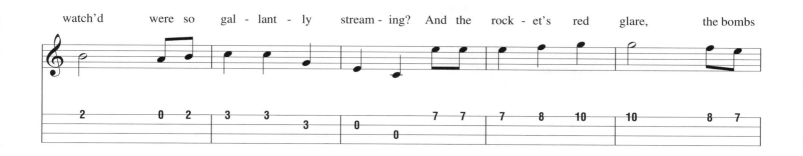

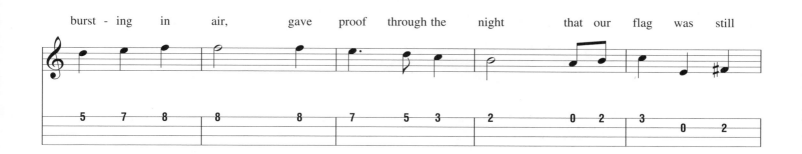

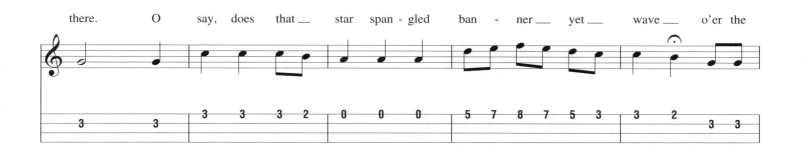

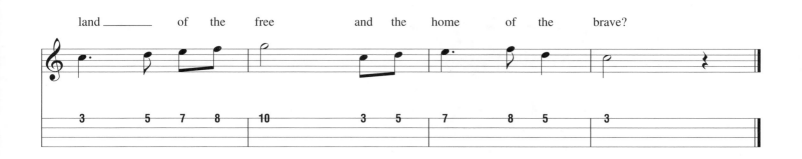

CHAPTER 3
STRUMMING CHORDS

The **chord diagrams** below on the left represent the ukulele fingerboard. The vertical lines are the strings and the horizontal lines are the frets. When an "o" appears on top of a string, it is played open. A solid black dot shows where to put your finger(s) for the chord.

A Minor Chord

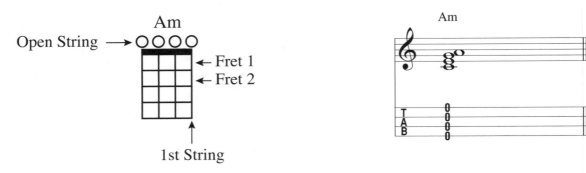

C Chord

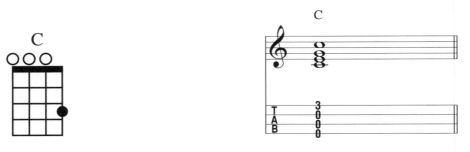

The **repeat signs** found in this example tell you to play the music again.

A Minor to C Chord Progression

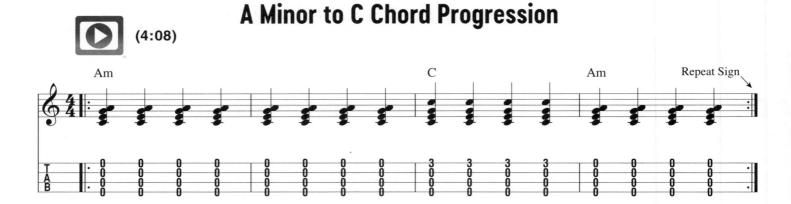

CHAPTER 4
ONE-FINGER CHORDS

C Major 7 Chord

 (0:48)

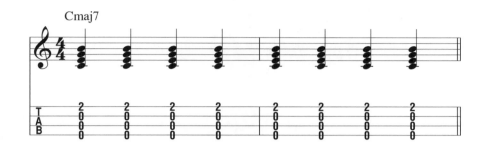

C7 Chord

 (1:08)

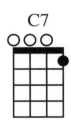

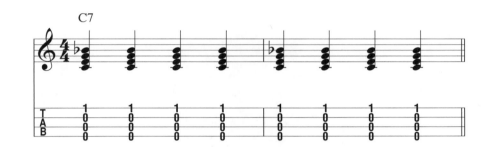

Pop Chord Progression

 (1:34)

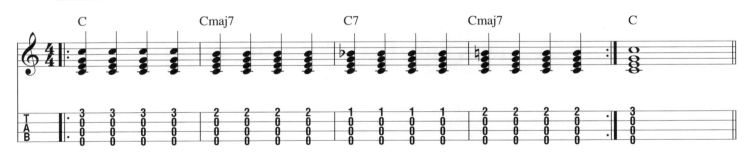

F Chord

 (2:02)

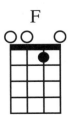

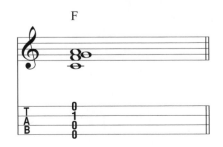

Eensy Weensy Spider

 (3:00)

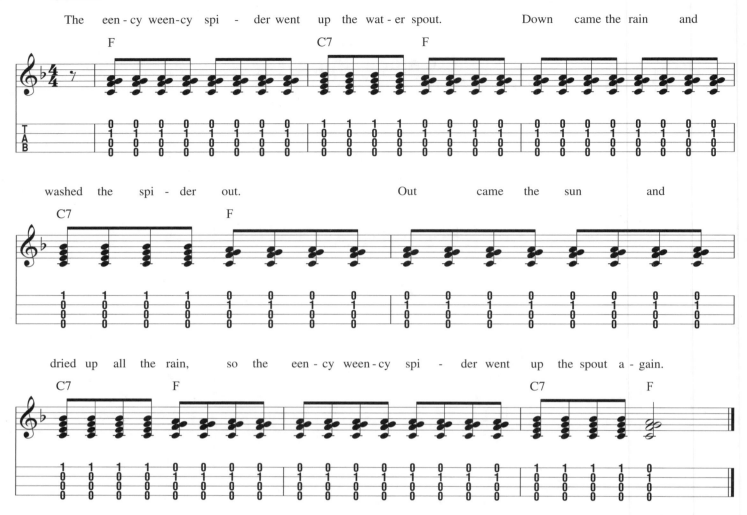

Row, Row, Row Your Boat

 (3:45)

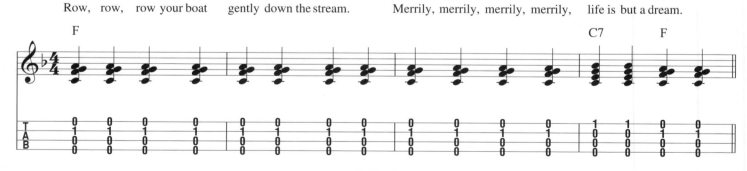

A Minor Chord

 **(4:28)**

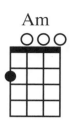
Am

A7 Chord

 **(4:48)**

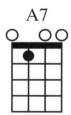
A7

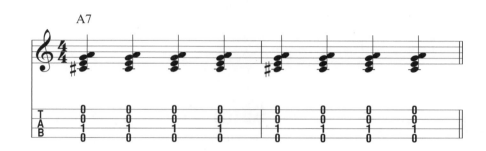

A7 Suspended Chord

 **(5:15)**

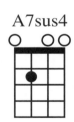
A7sus4

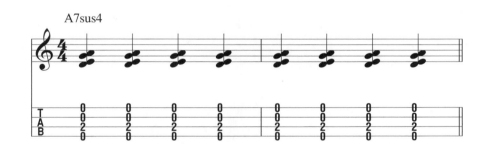

A7 to A7sus4 Chord Progression

 **(6:02)**

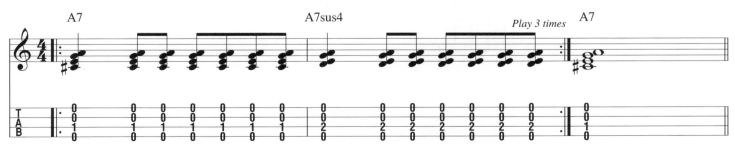

CHAPTER 5
TWO-FINGER CHORDS

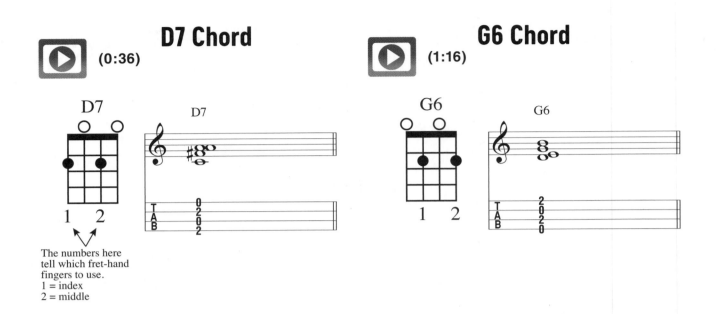

D7 Chord

▶ (0:36)

G6 Chord

▶ (1:16)

The numbers here tell which fret-hand fingers to use.
1 = index
2 = middle

G6 to D7 Progression

▶ (2:12)

A7 Flat 9 Chord

▶ (2:36)

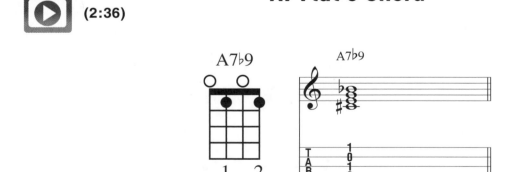

Chord Progression with A7♭9

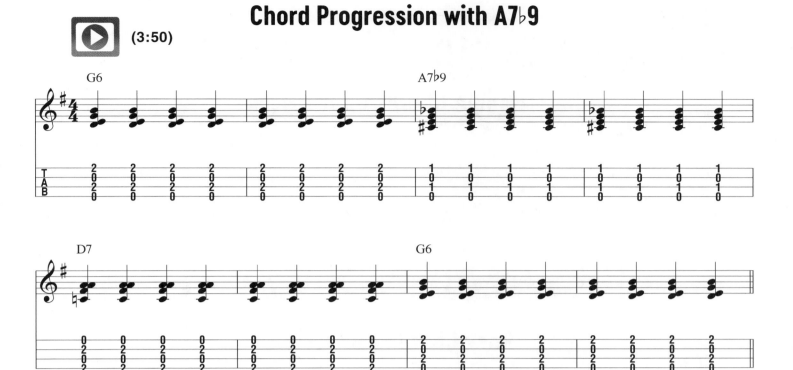

(3:50)

This next example contains **ending brackets**. On the first time through, play the 1st ending measure and repeat back to the start. On the second time through, skip the 1st ending and play the 2nd ending measure only.

"Crazy G" Chord Progression

(5:02)

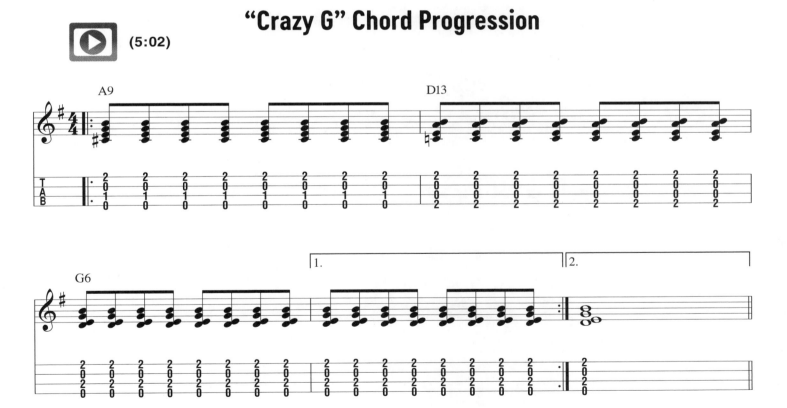

CHAPTER 6

THREE-FINGER "TRIANGLE" CHORDS

Triangle Chords Up the Neck

(2:32)

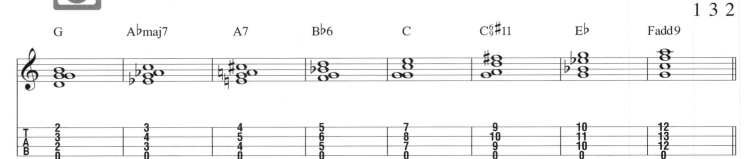

Rock Chord Progression

(5:40)

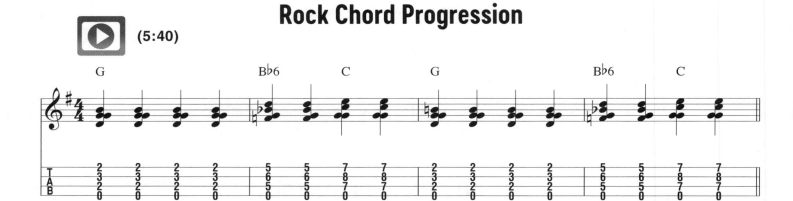

Happy Birthday to You

(7:24)

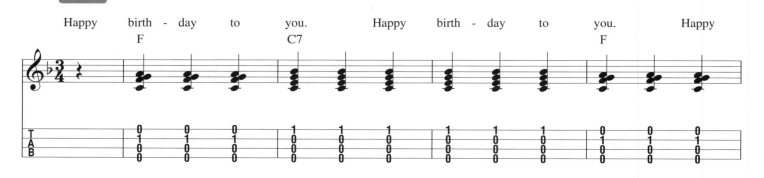

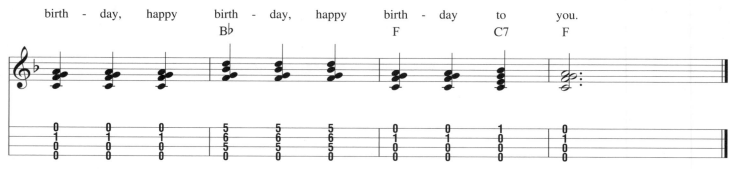

Silent Night

Words by Joseph Mohr
Translated by John F. Young
Music by Franz X. Gruber

Pop Chord Progression

(9:42)

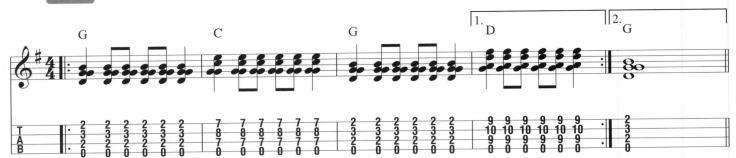

Descending Chord Progression

(10:54)

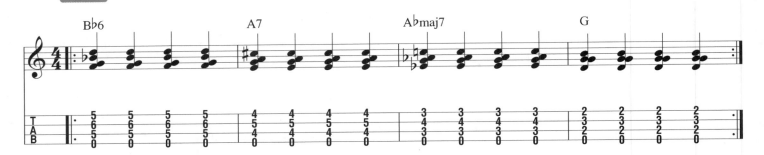

Descending Chords, Part 2

(12:44)

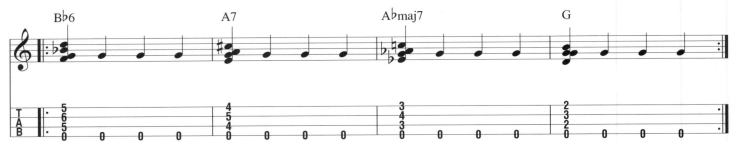

CHAPTER 7
THREE-FINGER "REVERSE-TRIANGLE" CHORDS

G7 Chord

C7 Chord

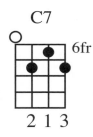

G to C7 Chord Progression

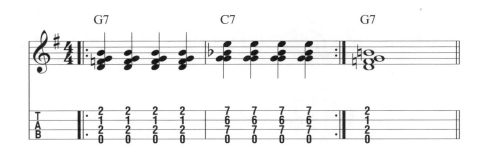

D7 Chord

 (2:32)

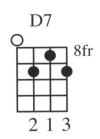

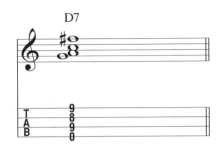

Blues Progression

 (3:16)

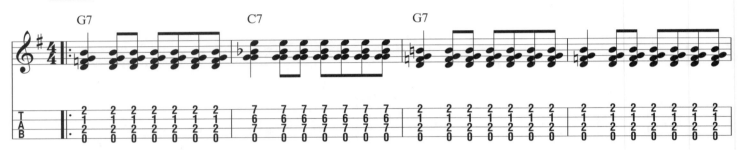

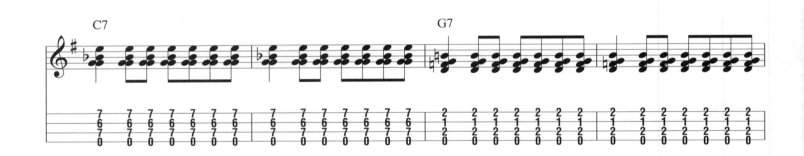

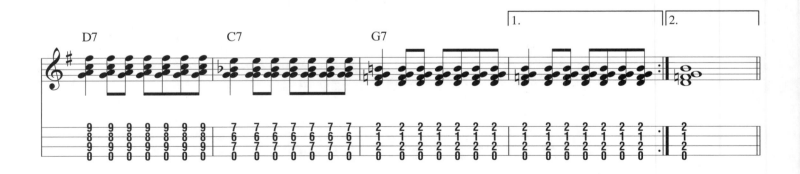

Twinkle, Twinkle Little Star

 (5:02)

CHAPTER 8
"STAIRS" CHORDS

E Minor Chord

 (0:54)

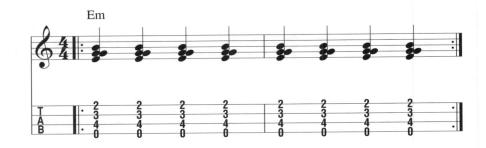

A Minor Chord

 (1:42)

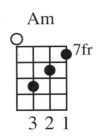

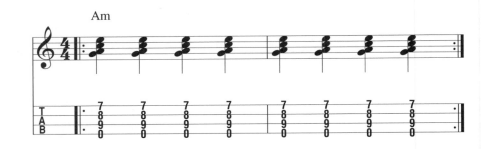

Em to Am Chord Progression

 (2:14)

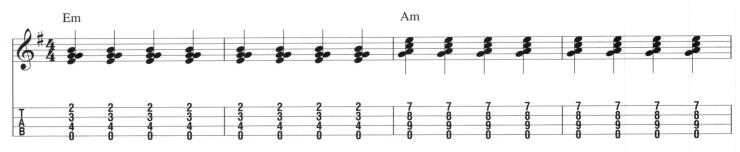

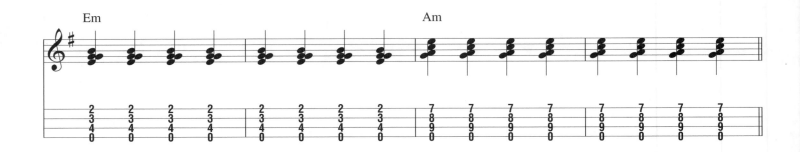

B7 Chord

 (2:52)

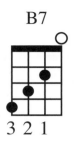

Em to B7 Chord Progression

 (4:08)

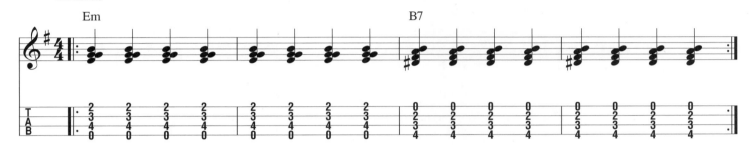

C6 Chord

 (4:33)

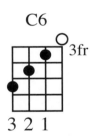

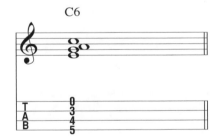

B7 to C6 Chord Progression

 (5:16)

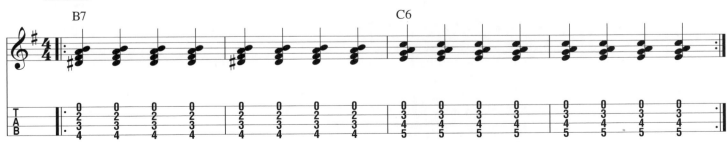

Pipeline
Chords

 (6:48)

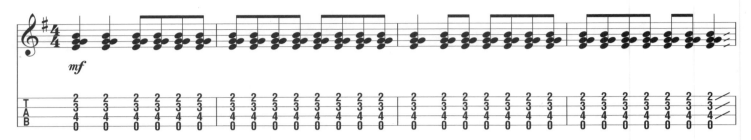

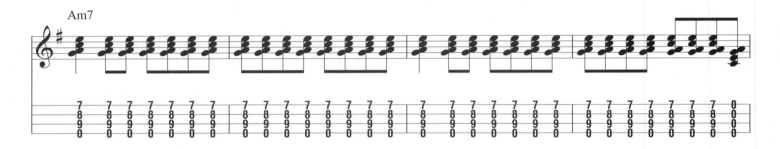

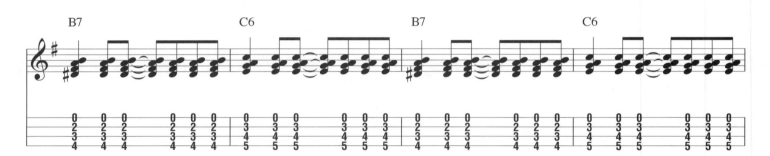

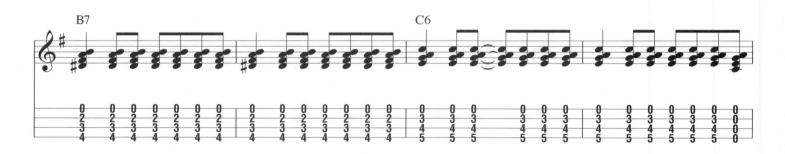

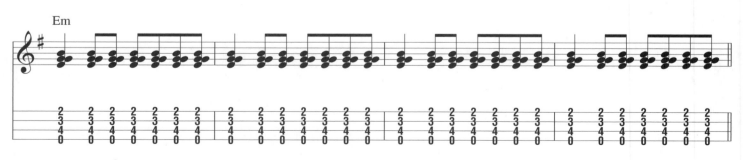

CHAPTER 9
POPULAR CHORD PROGRESSIONS

Chord Progression 1

(0:24)

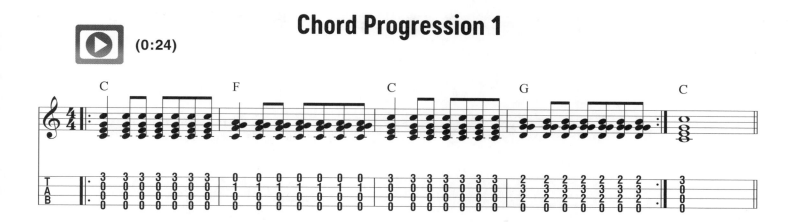

Chord Progression 2

(1:00)

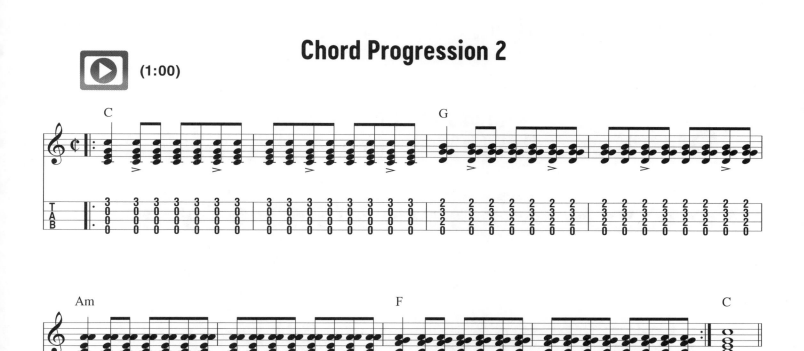

Chord Progression 3

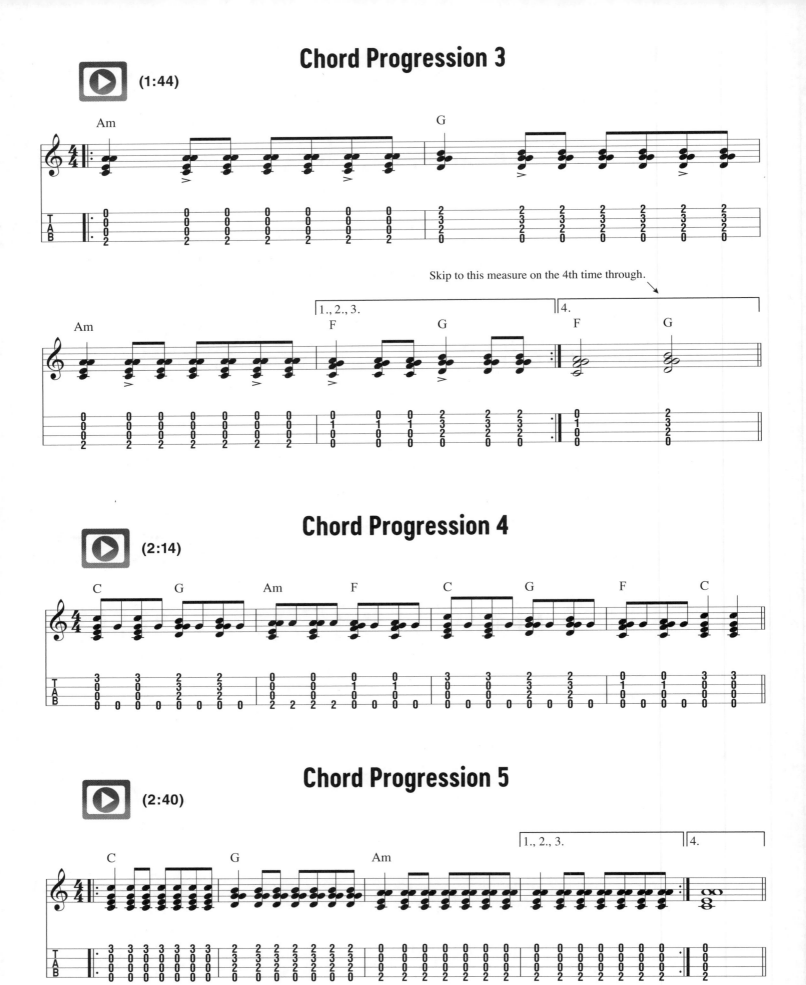

Skip to this measure on the 4th time through.

Chord Progression 4

Chord Progression 5

26

CHAPTER 10
PICKING WITH THUMB AND FINGERS

Exercise 1

Exercise 2

Arpeggiated Chords

An arpeggio is a chord's individual notes played in succession. In this example, I pick the arpeggios of the C and F chords using my thumb and various fingers of my right hand. The fingers used to pick each note are shown below using the traditional *p-i-m-a* notation:

p = thumb, *i* = index finger, *m* = middle, *a* = ring

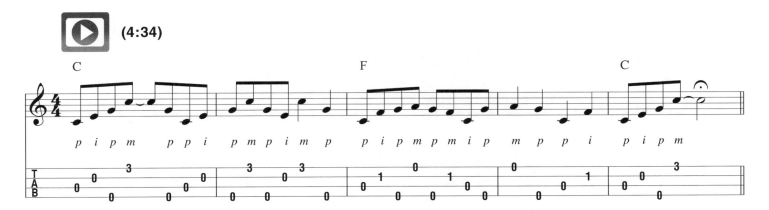

Ave Maria

 (5:13)

Freely

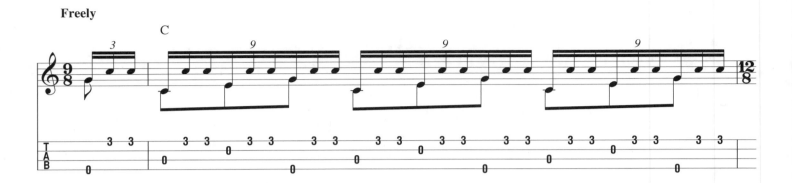

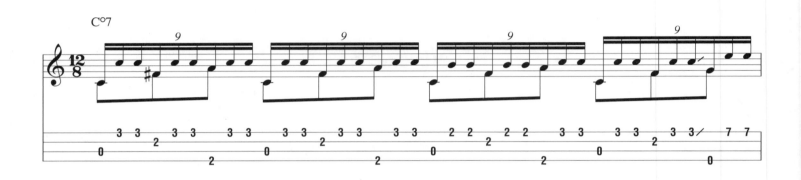

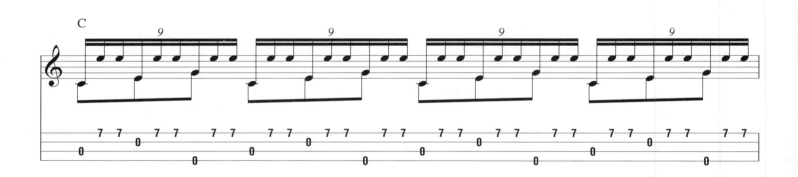

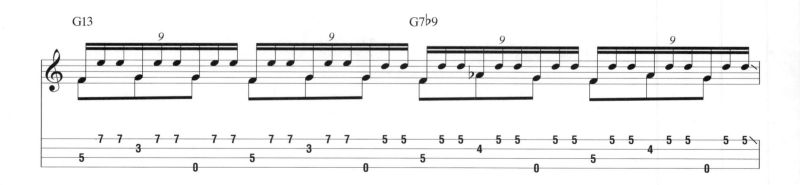

By Franz Schubert
Copyright © 2017 by HAL LEONARD LLC
International Copyright Secured All Rights Reserved

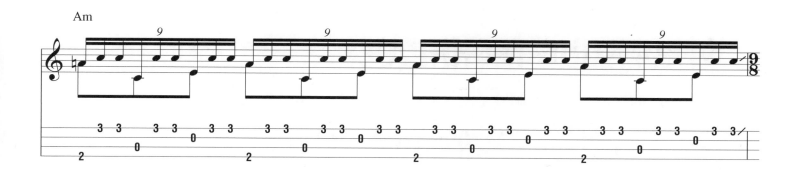

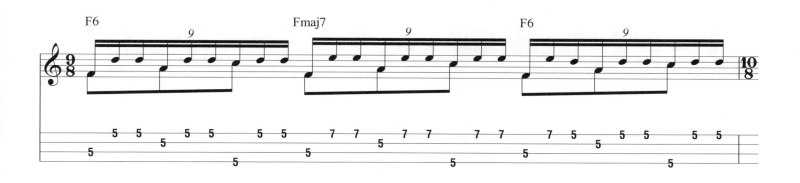

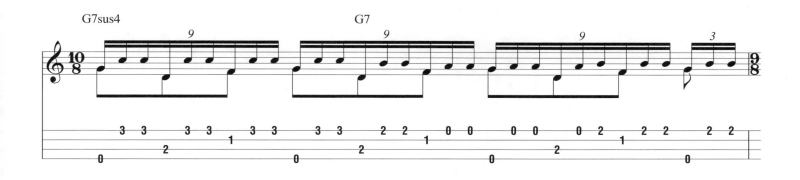

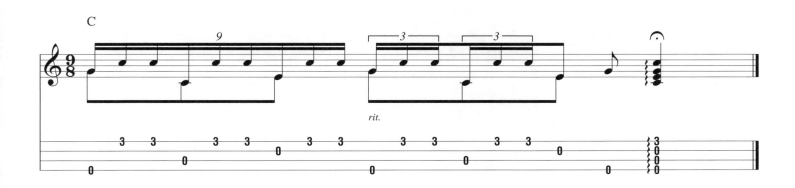

CHAPTER 11
STRUMMING TECHNIQUES

⊓ = downstroke   ∨ = upstroke

Quarter Notes

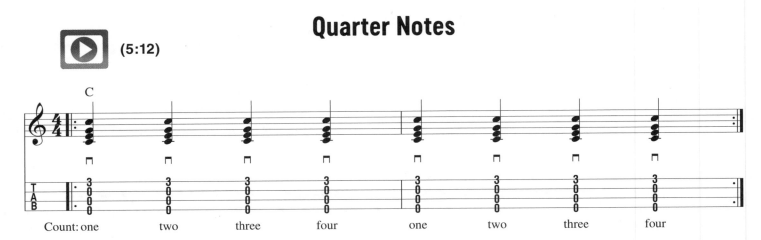

Eighth Notes

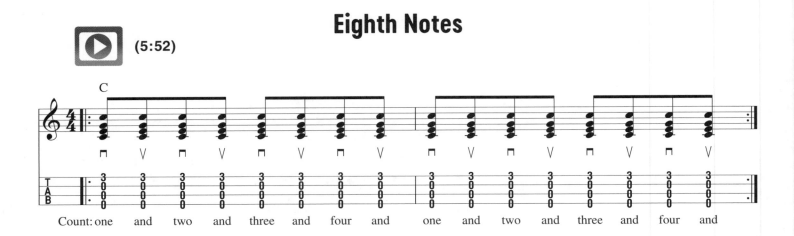

Sixteenth Notes

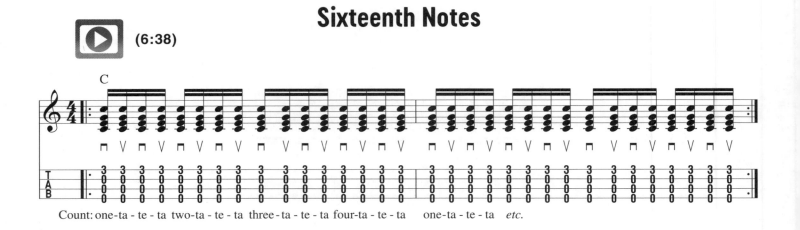

CHAPTER 12
TREMOLO PICKING

Tremolo picking is a technique performed by picking a note rapidly and continuously. The symbol ≣ is found above or below a note that is tremolo picked.

Tremolo Example

Here's a melodic excerpt from the song "Travels" for fun practicing the tremolo picking technique. See page 53 for the full song transcription.

Travels

Written by Jake Shimabukuro
Copyright © 2015 Uke Ox Publishing (BMI)
All Rights Reserved   Used by Permission

CHAPTER 13
WHILE MY GUITAR GENTLY WEEPS

While My Guitar Gently Weeps
Chords

BONUS SONG TRANSCRIPTIONS
Celtic Tune

**From Chapter 10
(6:20)**

A

Moderately fast ♩ = 144

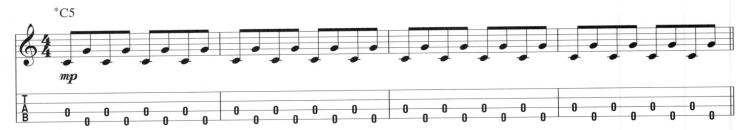

*Chord symbols reflect implied harmony.

𝄋 B

**2nd time, w/ octave pedal, set for one octave higher, next 29 meas.
***3rd time, w/ palm mute, next 12 meas.

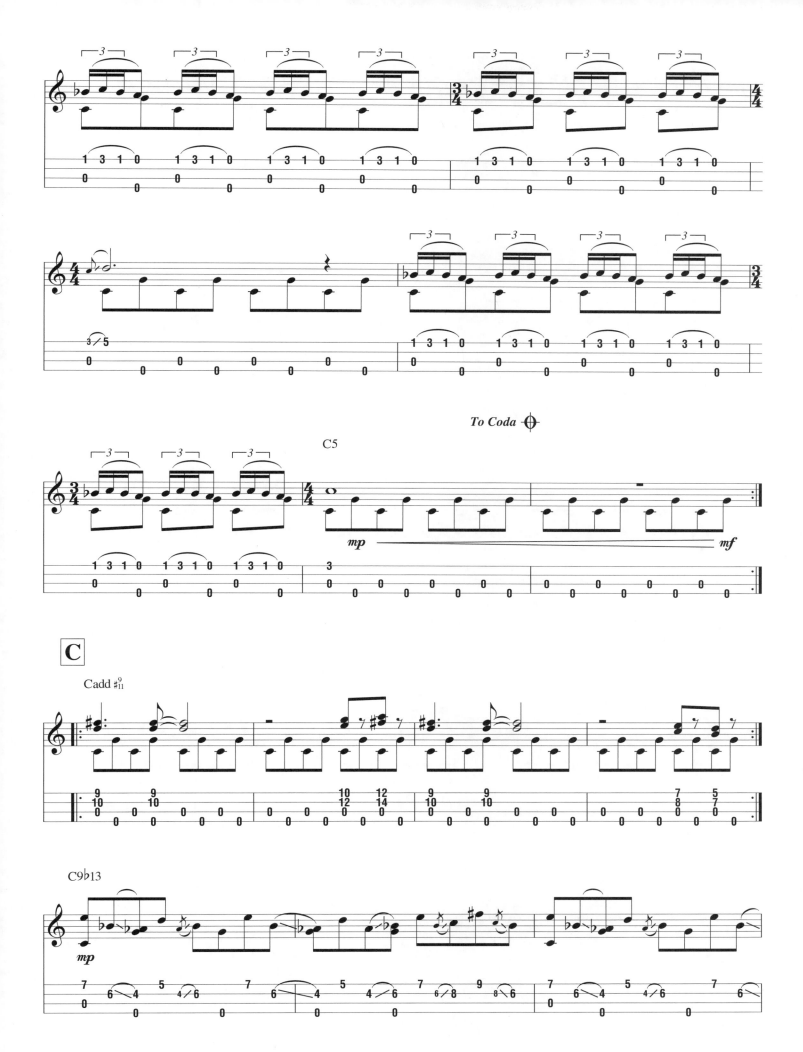

Dragon

From "Gear" Lesson
(3:46)

 A

Fast ♩ = 152

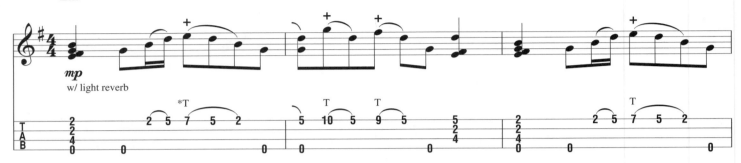

*Tapping: Hammer ("tap") the fret indicated w/ pick-hand
index finger and pull off to the next note fretted by the fret hand.

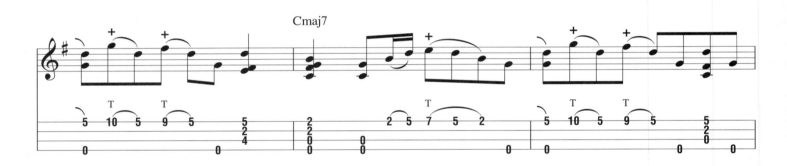

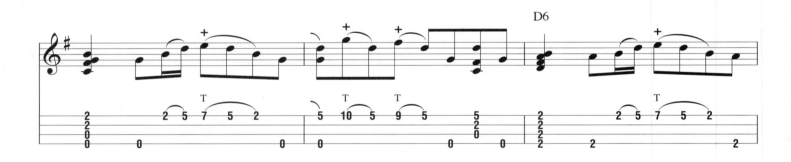

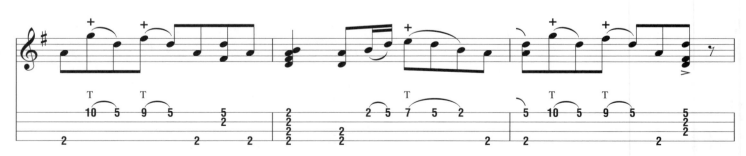

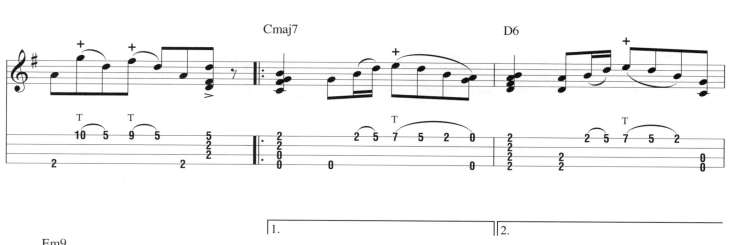

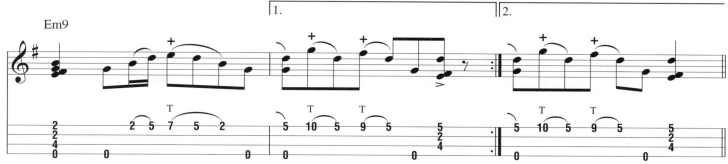

D

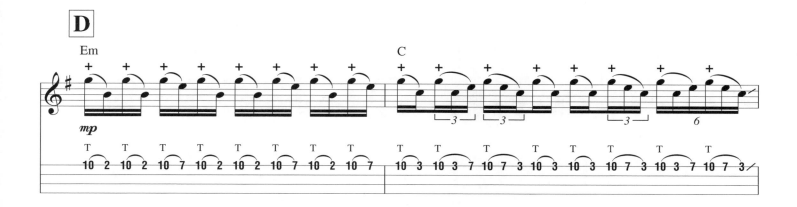

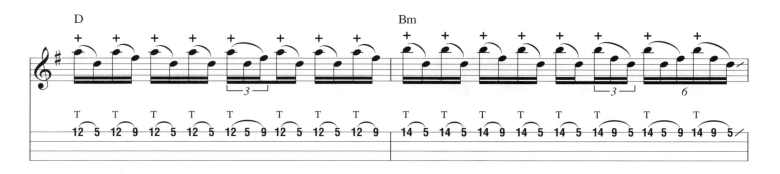

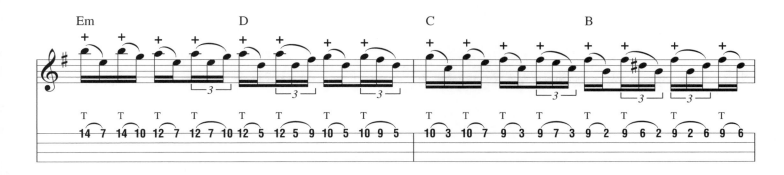

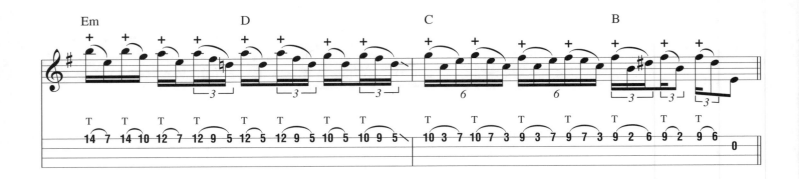

E

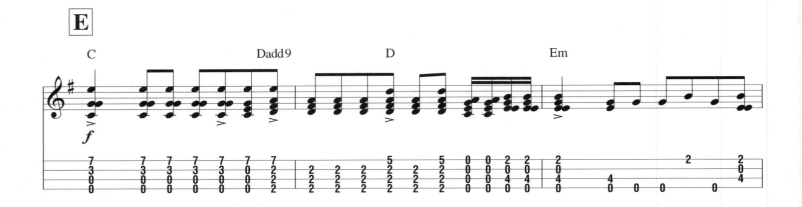

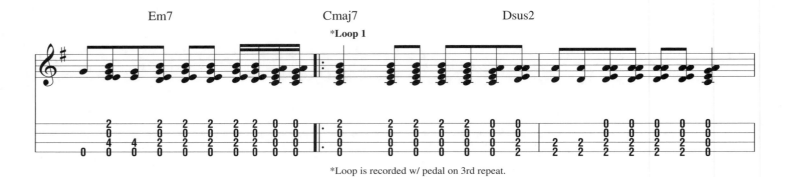

*Loop is recorded w/ pedal on 3rd repeat.

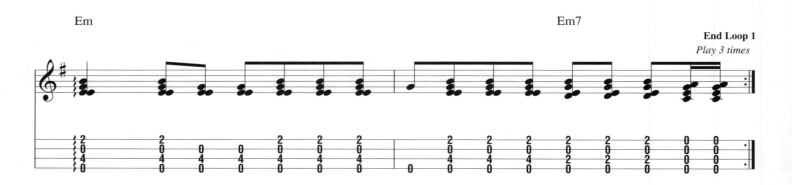

Cont. Loop 1 regeneration (8 times)

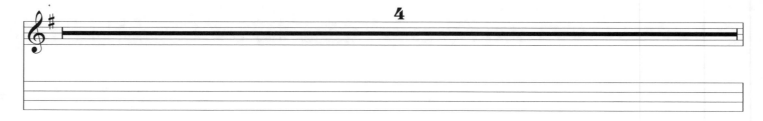

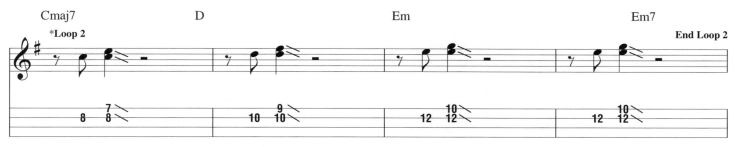

*Created using Loop pedal.

Cont. Loop regeneration (6 times)

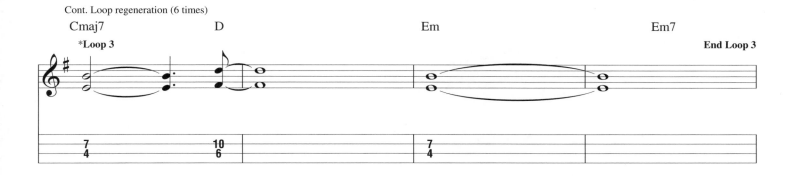

Cont. Loop 3 regeneration (5 times)

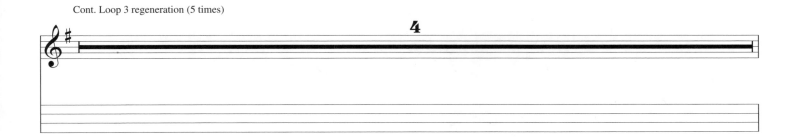

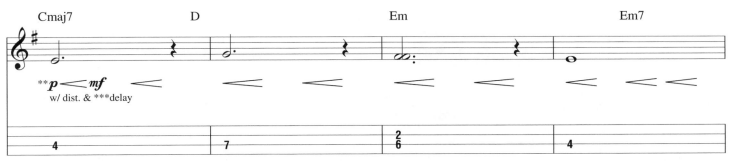

**Vol. swells w/ volume pedal
        ***Set for quarter-note regeneration w/ 4 repeats.

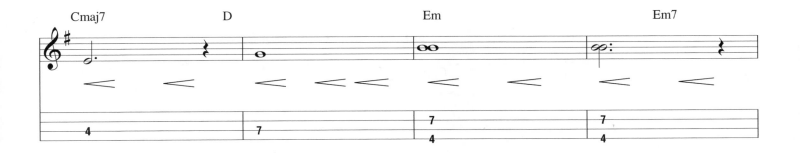

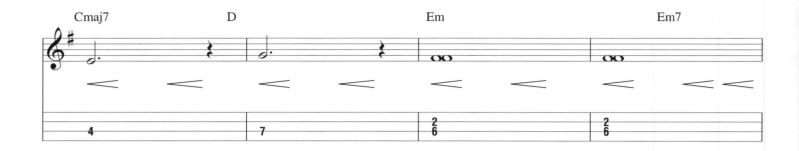

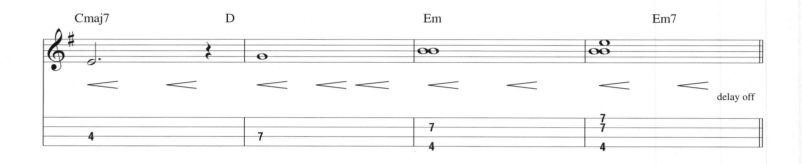

F

Cont. Loops 1, 2 & 3 (19 1/2 times)

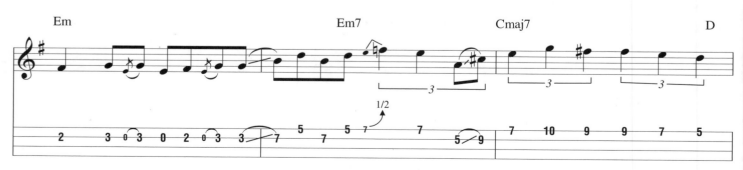

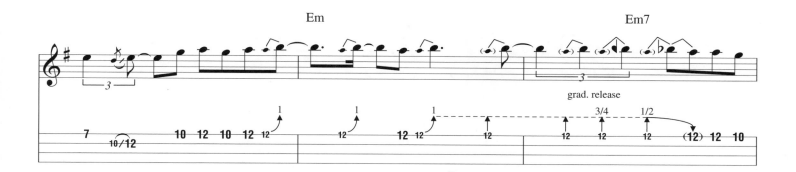

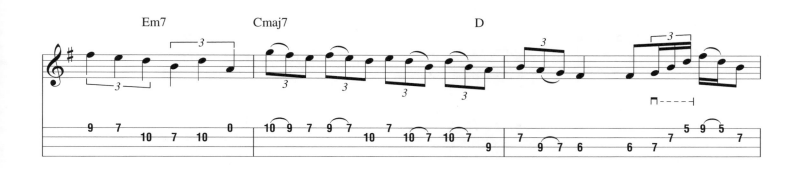

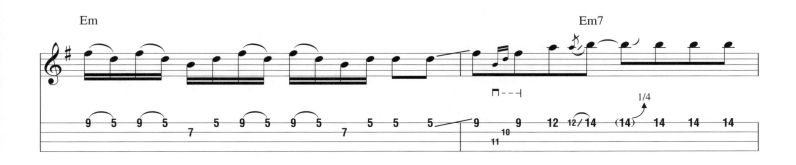

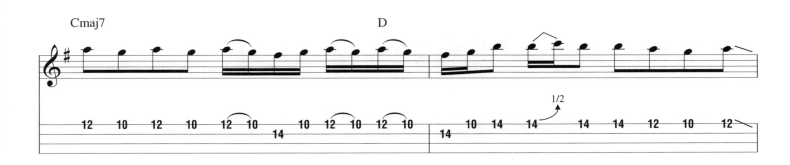

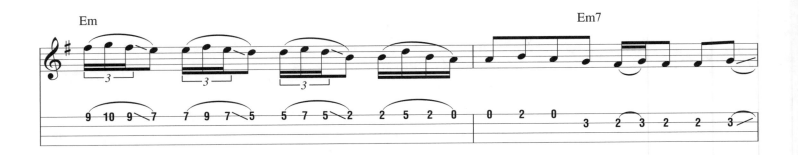

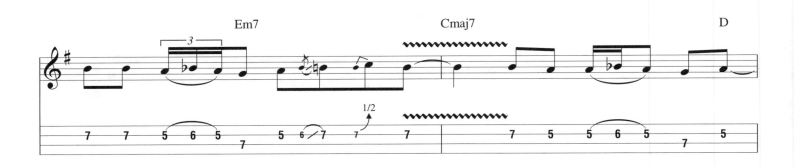

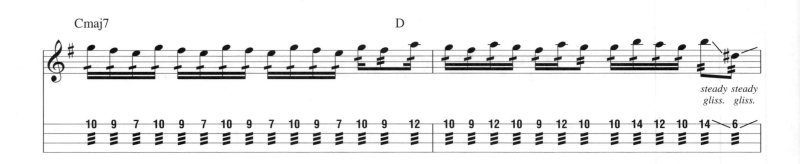

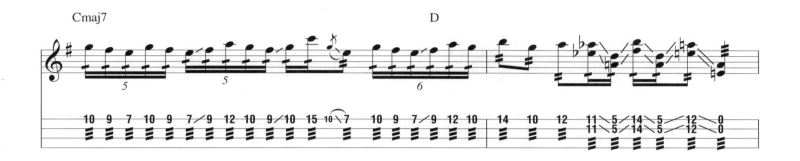

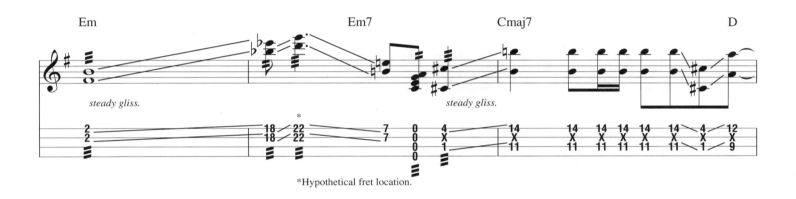

*Hypothetical fret location.

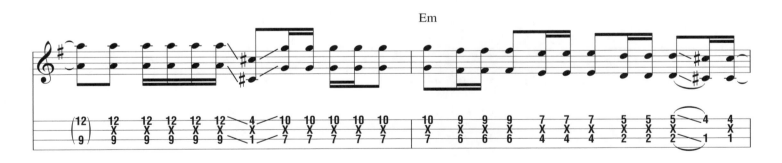

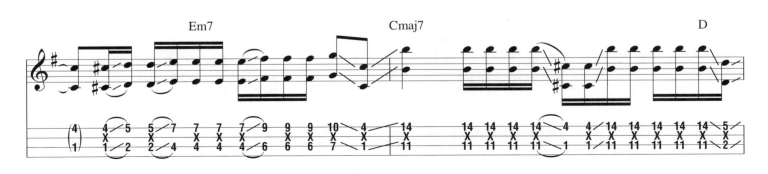

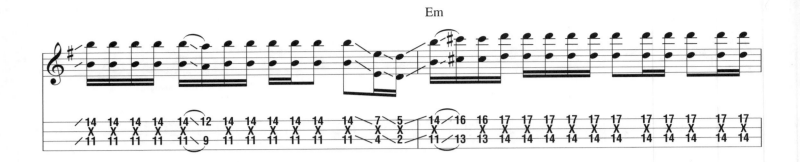

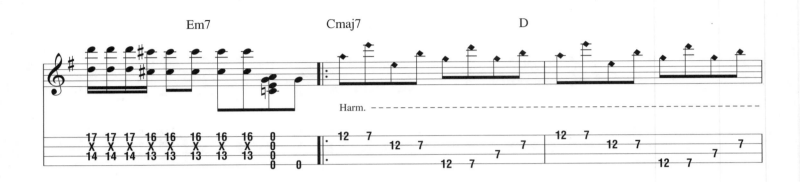

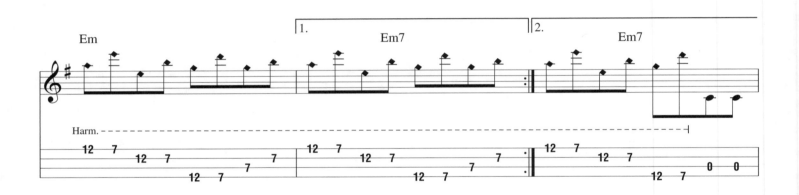

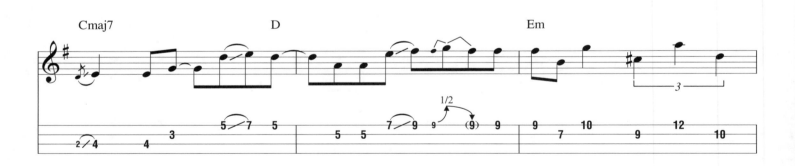

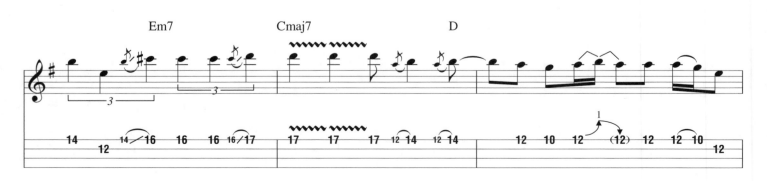

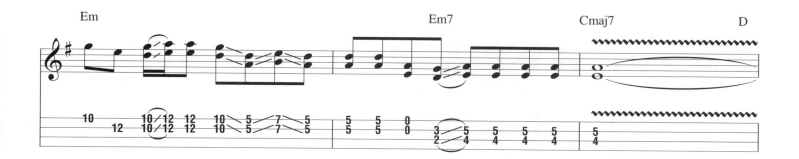
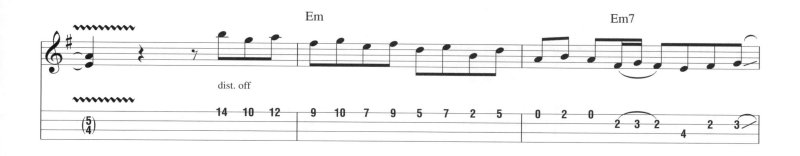
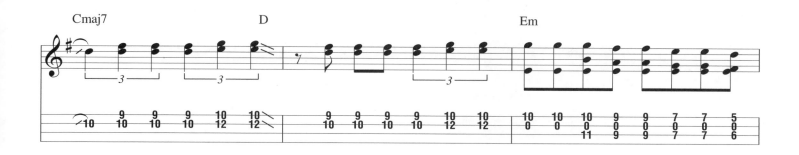
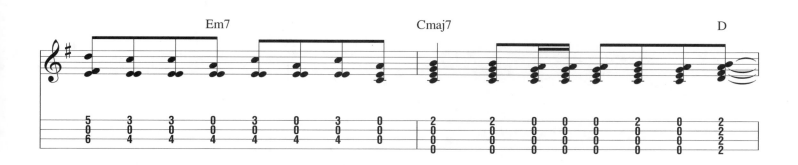
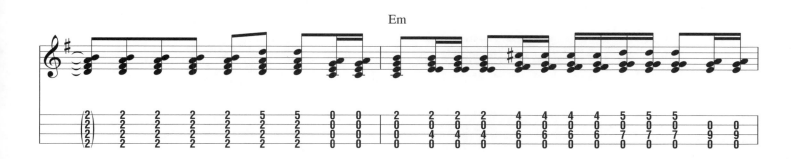

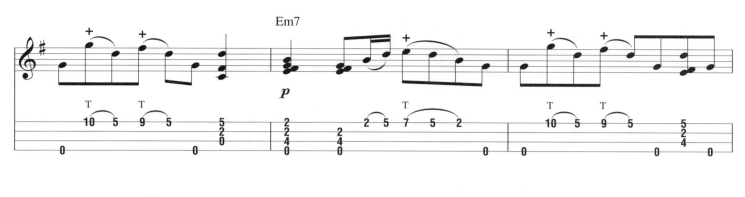

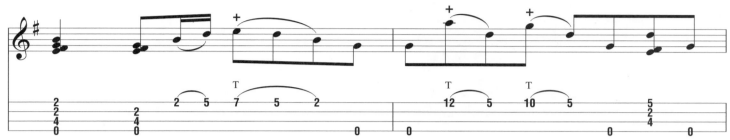

*Harp Harm.: Lightly touch string at
fret number in parentheses w/ pick-hand
index finger while simultaneously
picking fretted or open note.

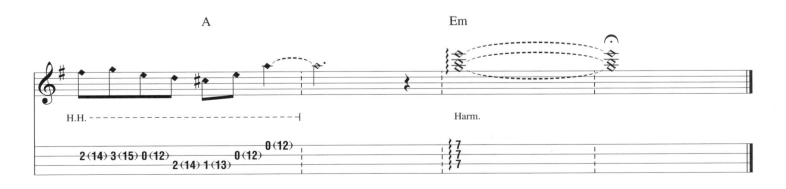

Pipeline

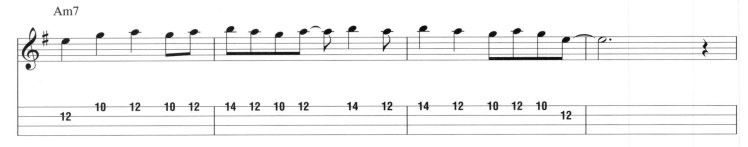

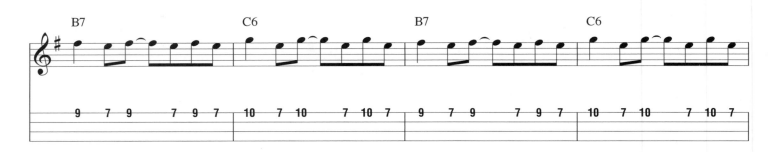

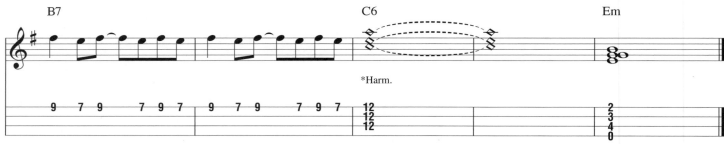

*Harm.

*Harmonic: Strike the notes while fret-hand finger
lightly touches the strings directly over the 12th fret.

Travels

**From Chapter 12
(0:50)**

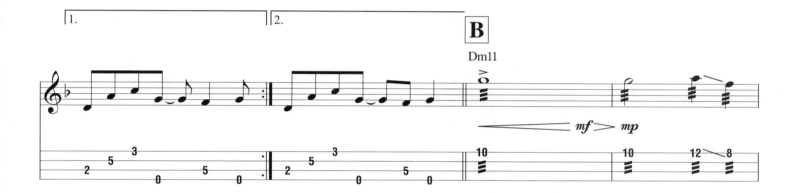

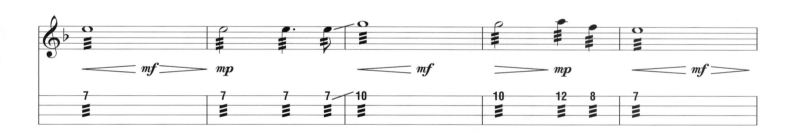

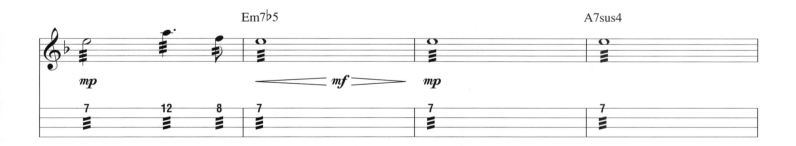

Written by Jake Shimabukuro
Copyright © 2015 Uke Ox Publishing (BMI)
All Rights Reserved   Used by Permission

D

*Dm7

*Chord symbol reflects basic harmony.

**Played behind the beat.

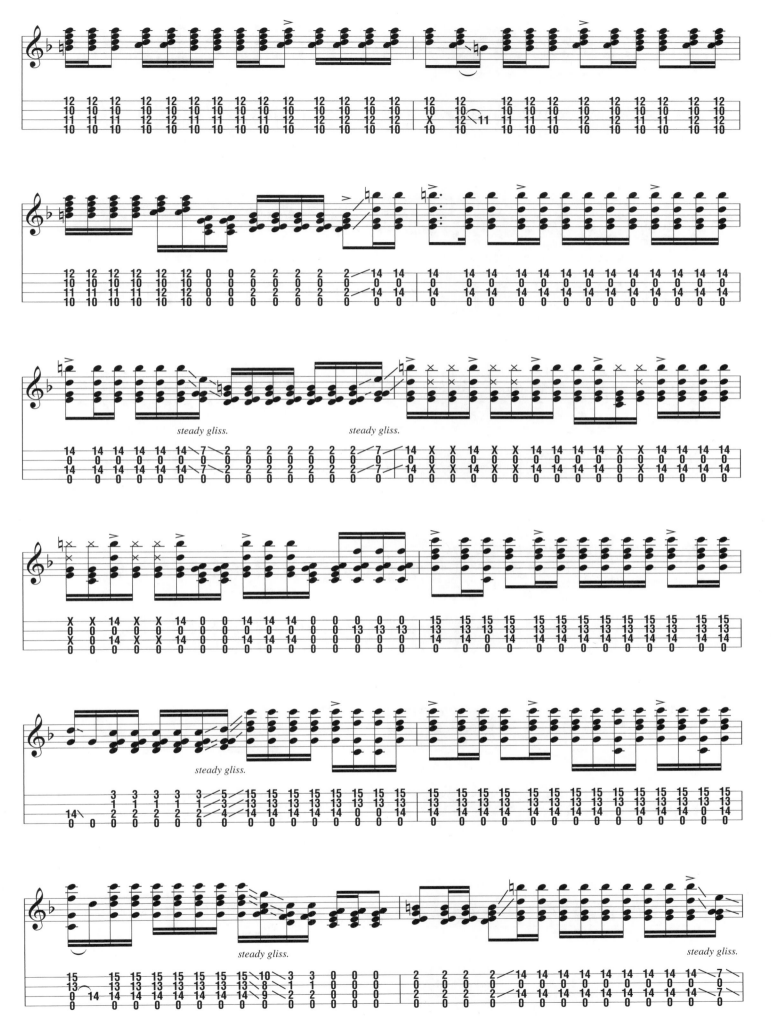

*Refers to first & second strings only,
throughout.

From Chapter 11
(3:10)

Ukulele Five-O

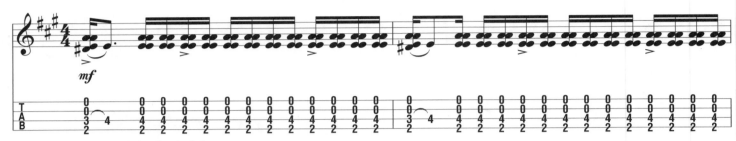

*Chord symbols reflect basic harmony.

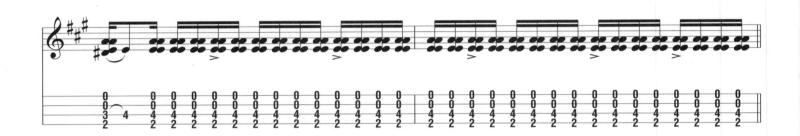

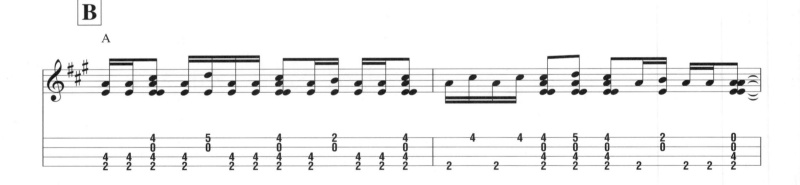

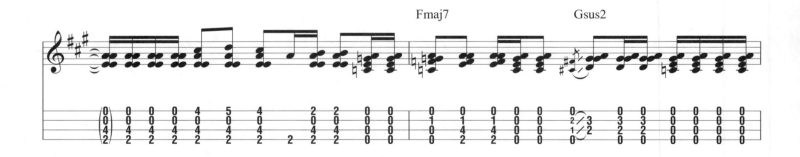

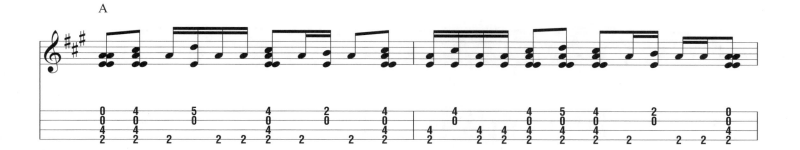

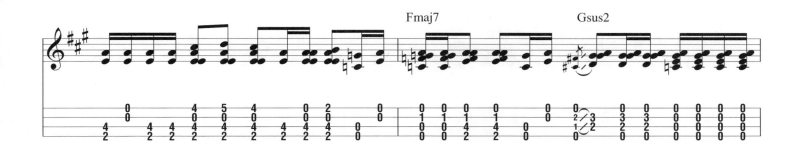

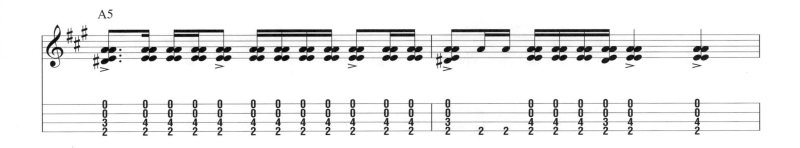

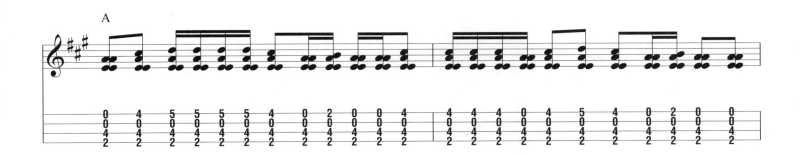

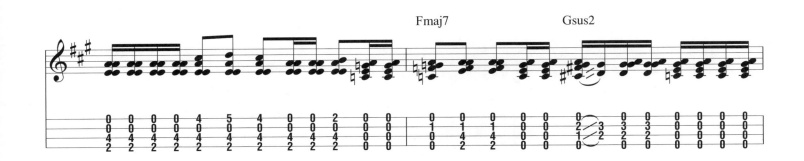

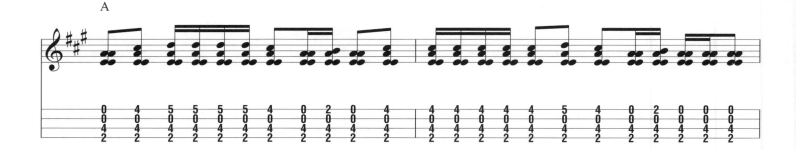

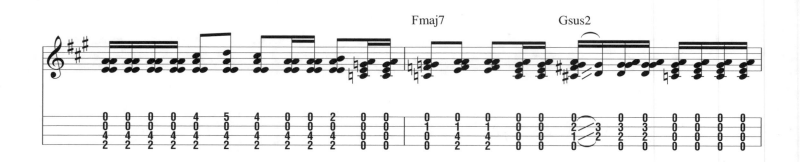

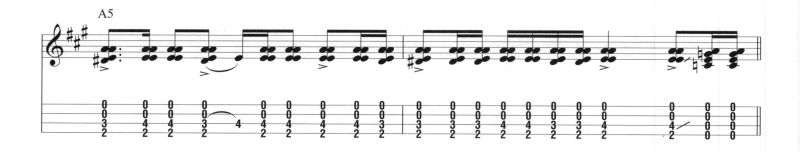

Gmaj7sus2

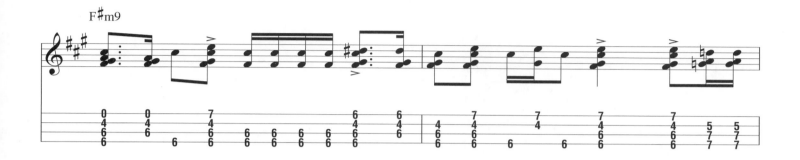

F#m9

Gmaj7sus2

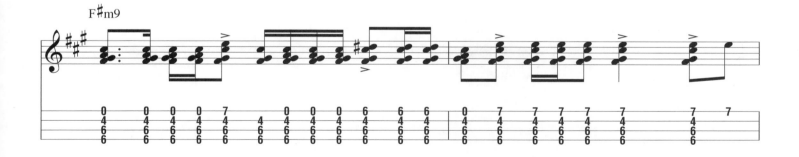

F#m9

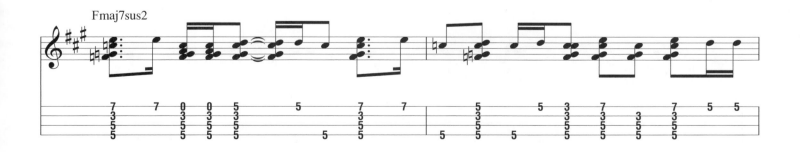

Fmaj7sus2

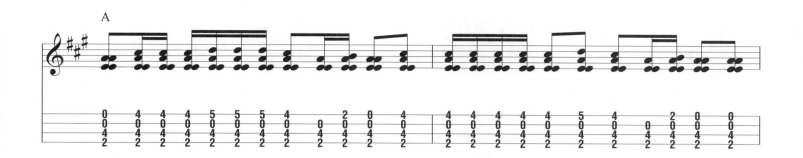

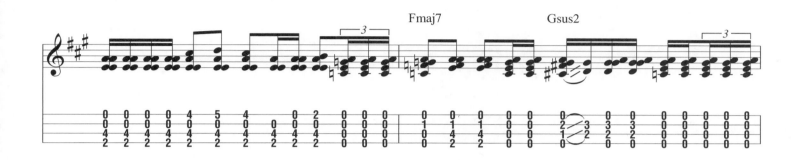

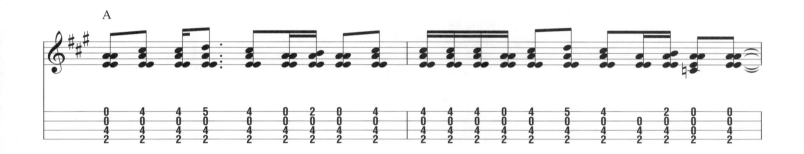

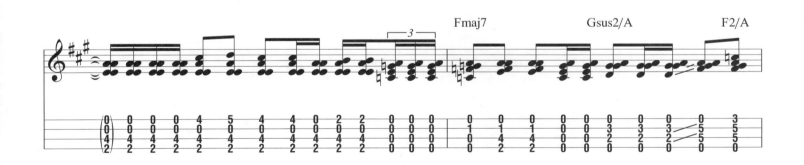

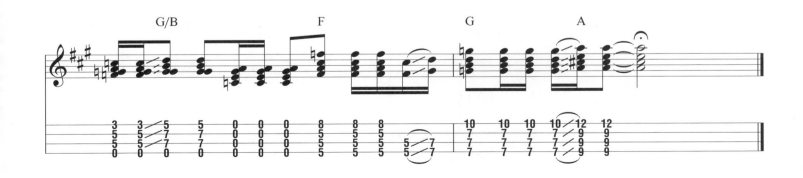

While My Guitar Gently Weeps

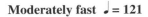From Chapter 13
(4:50)

A

Moderately fast ♩ = 121

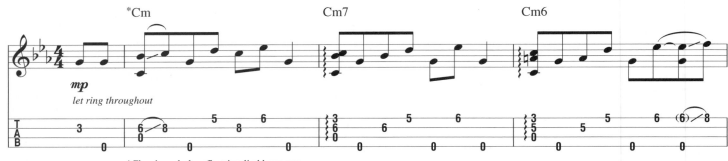

*Chord symbols reflect implied harmony.

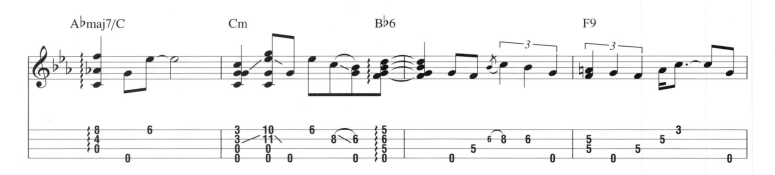

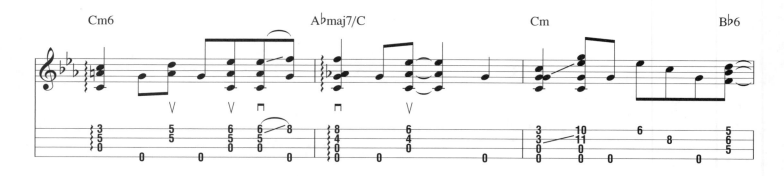

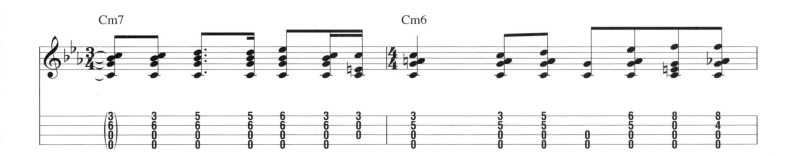

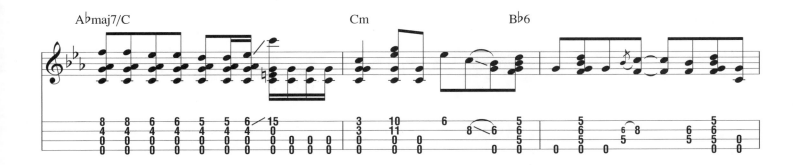

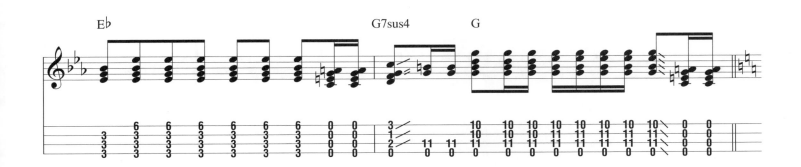

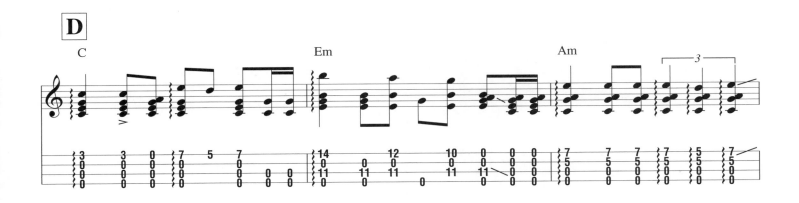

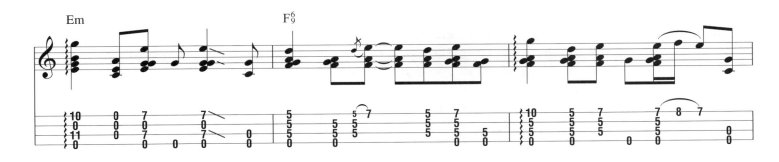

Cm6

A♭maj7/C

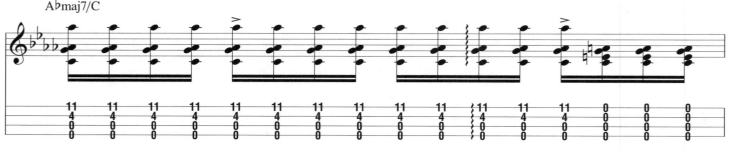

Cm

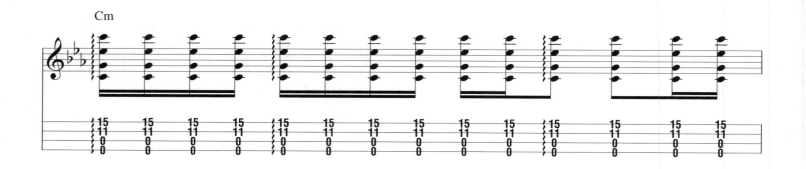

Cm7/B♭

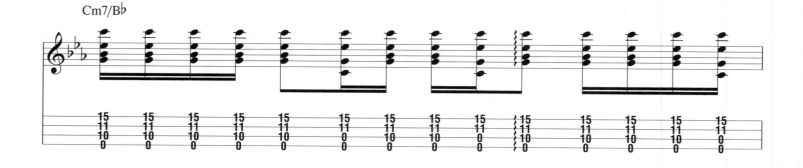

Cm6/A

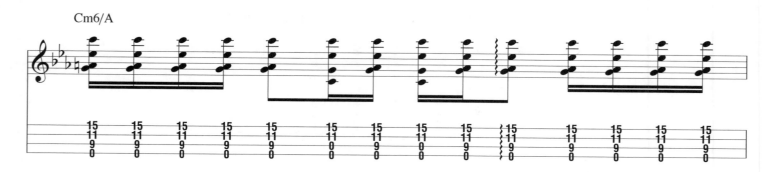

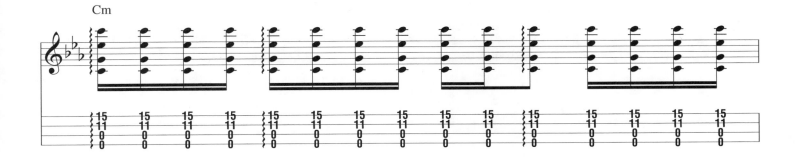

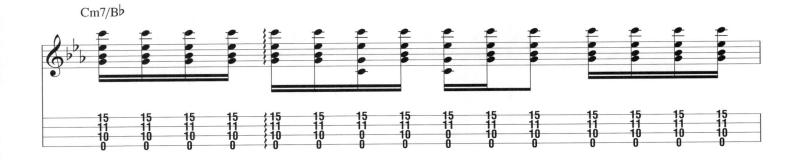

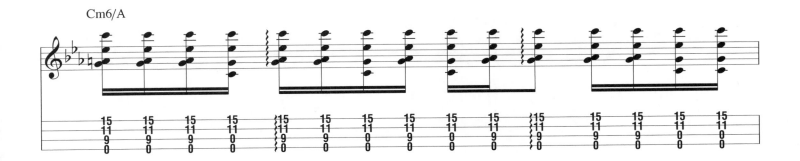

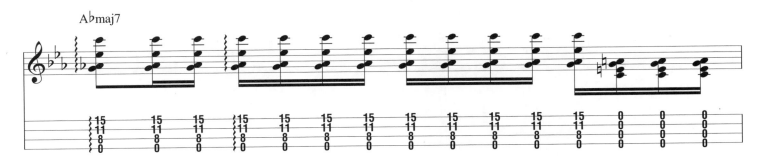

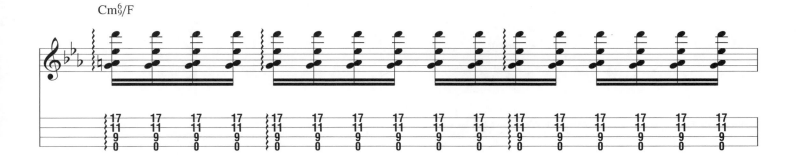

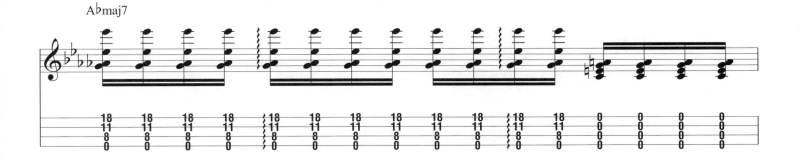

*Hit strings w/ open hand.

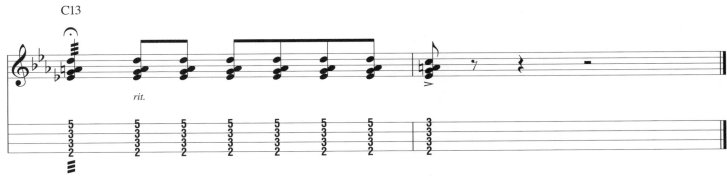

UKULELE NOTATION LEGEND

THE MUSICAL STAFF shows pitches and rhythms and is divided by bar lines into measures. Pitches are named after the first seven letters of the alphabet.

TABLATURE graphically represents the ukulele fingerboard. Each horizontal line represents a a string, and each number represents a fret.

2nd string, 3rd fret   1st & 2nd strings open, played together   open F chord

HALF-STEP BEND: Strike the note and bend up 1/2 step.

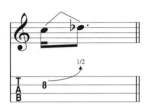

WHOLE-STEP BEND: Strike the note and bend up one step.

GRACE NOTE BEND: Strike the note and immediately bend up as indicated.

SLIGHT (MICROTONE) BEND: Strike the note and bend up 1/4 step.

BEND AND RELEASE: Strike the note and bend up as indicated, then release back to the original note. Only the first note is struck.

PRE-BEND: Bend the note as indicated, then strike it.

VIBRATO: The string is vibrated by rapidly bending and releasing the note with the fretting hand.

HAMMER-ON: Strike the first (lower) note with one finger, then sound the higher note (on the same string) with another finger by fretting it without picking.

PULL-OFF: Place both fingers on the notes to be sounded. Strike the first note and without picking, pull the finger off to sound the second (lower) note.

LEGATO SLIDE: Strike the first note and then slide the same fret-hand finger up or down to the second note. The second note is not struck.

SHIFT SLIDE: Same as legato slide, except the second note is struck.

TRILL: Very rapidly alternate between the notes indicated by continuously hammering on and pulling off.

TREMOLO PICKING: The note is picked as rapidly and continuously as possible.

Additional Musical Definitions

	(accent)	• Accentuate note (play it louder)
	(staccato)	• Play the note short
D.S. al Coda		• Go back to the sign (𝄋), then play until the measure marked "***To Coda***," then skip to the section labelled "**Coda**."
D.C. al Fine		• Go back to the beginning of the song and play until the measure marked "***Fine***" (end).
N.C.		• No chord.
		• Repeat measures between signs.
1. 2.		• When a repeated section has different endings, play the first ending only the first time and the second ending only the second time.

NOTE: Tablature numbers in parentheses mean:

1. The note is being sustained over a system (note in standard notation is tied), or

2. The note is sustained, but a new articulation (such as a hammer-on, pull-off, slide or vibrato) begins, or

3. The note is a barely audible "ghost" note (note in standard notation is also in parentheses).

Ride the Ukulele Wave!

The Beach Boys for Ukulele

This folio features 20 favorites, including: Barbara Ann • Be True to Your School • California Girls • Fun, Fun, Fun • God Only Knows • Good Vibrations • Help Me Rhonda • I Get Around • In My Room • Kokomo • Little Deuce Coupe • Sloop John B • Surfin' U.S.A. • Wouldn't It Be Nice • and more!

00701726 . . . . $14.99

Disney Songs for Ukulele

20 great Disney classics arranged for all uke players, including: Beauty and the Beast • Bibbidi-Bobbidi-Boo (The Magic Song) • Can You Feel the Love Tonight • Chim Chim Cher-ee • Heigh-Ho • It's a Small World • Some Day My Prince Will Come • We're All in This Together • When You Wish upon a Star • and more.

00701708 . . . . $14.99

Jack Johnson – Strum & Sing

Cherry Lane Music
Strum along with 41 Jack Johnson songs using this top-notch collection of chords and lyrics just for the uke! Includes: Better Together • Bubble Toes • Cocoon • Do You Remember • Flake • Fortunate Fool • Good People • Holes to Heaven • Taylor • Tomorrow Morning • and more.

02501702 . . . . $15.99

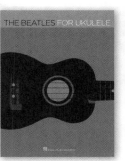

The Beatles for Ukulele

Ukulele players can strum, sing and pick along with 20 Beatles classics! Includes: All You Need Is Love • Eight Days a Week • Good Day Sunshine • Here, There and Everywhere • Let It Be • Love Me Do • Penny Lane • Yesterday • and more.

00700154 . . . . $16.99

First 50 Songs You Should Play on Ukulele

An amazing collection of 50 accessible, must-know favorites: Edelweiss • Hey, Soul Sister • I Walk the Line • I'm Yours • Imagine • Over the Rainbow • Peaceful Easy Feeling • The Rainbow Connection • Riptide • and many more.

00149250 . . . . $14.99

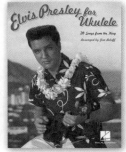

Elvis Presley for Ukulele

arr. Jim Beloff
20 classic hits from The King: All Shook Up • Blue Hawaii • Blue Suede Shoes • Can't Help Falling in Love • Don't • Heartbreak Hotel • Hound Dog • Jailhouse Rock • Love Me • Love Me Tender • Return to Sender • Suspicious Minds • Teddy Bear • and more.

00701004 . . . . $15.99

The Daily Ukulele

compiled and arranged by Liz and Jim Beloff
Strum a different song everyday with easy arrangements of 365 of your favorite songs in one big songbook! Includes favorites by the Beatles, Beach Boys, and Bob Dylan, folk songs, pop songs, kids' songs, Christmas carols, and Broadway and Hollywood tunes, all with a spiral binding for ease of use.

00240356 . . . . $39.99

Folk Songs for Ukulele

A great collection to take along to the campfire! 60 folk songs, including: Amazing Grace • Buffalo Gals • Camptown Races • For He's a Jolly Good Fellow • Good Night Ladies • Home on the Range • I've Been Working on the Railroad • Kumbaya • My Bonnie Lies over the Ocean • On Top of Old Smoky • Scarborough Fair • Swing Low, Sweet Chariot • Take Me Out to the Ball Game • Yankee Doodle • and more.

00696068 . . . . $12.99

Jake Shimabukuro – Peace Love Ukulele

Deemed "the Hendrix of the ukulele," Hawaii native Jake Shimabukuro is a uke virtuoso. Our songbook features note-for-note transcriptions with ukulele tablature of Jake's masterful playing on all the CD tracks: Bohemian Rhapsody • Boy Meets Girl • Bring Your Adz • Hallelujah • Pianoforte 2010 • Variation on a Dance 2010 • and more, plus two bonus selections!

00702516 . . . . $19.99

The Daily Ukulele – Leap Year Edition

366 More Songs for Better Living
compiled and arranged by Liz and Jim Beloff
An amazing second volume with 366 MORE songs for you to master each day of a leap year! Includes: Ain't No Sunshine • Calendar Girl • I Got You Babe • Lean on Me • Moondance • and many, many more.

00240681 . . . . $39.99

Hawaiian Songs for Ukulele

Over thirty songs from the state that made the ukulele famous, including: Beyond the Rainbow • Hanalei Moon • Ka-lu-a • Lovely Hula Girl • Mele Kalikimaka • One More Aloha • Sea Breeze • Tiny Bubbles • Waikiki • and more.

00696065 . . . . $10.99

Worship Songs for Ukulele

25 worship songs: Amazing Grace (My Chains are Gone) • Blessed Be Your Name • Enough • God of Wonders • Holy Is the Lord • How Great Is Our God • In Christ Alone • Love the Lord • Mighty to Save • Sing to the King • Step by Step • We Fall Down • and more.

00702546 . . . . $14.99

Disney characters and artwork © Disney Enterprises, Inc.

Prices, contents, and availability subject to change.

1216

UKULELE CHORD SONGBOOKS

This series features convenient 6" x 9" books with complete lyrics and chord symbols for dozens of great songs. Each song also includes chord grids at the top of every page and the first notes of the melody for easy reference.

ACOUSTIC ROCK

60 tunes: American Pie • Band on the Run • Catch the Wind • Daydream • Every Rose Has Its Thorn • Hallelujah • Iris • More Than Words • Patience • The Sound of Silence • Space Oddity • Sweet Talkin' Woman • Wake up Little Susie • Who'll Stop the Rain • and more.
00702482 . . . . $14.99

THE BEATLES

100 favorites: Across the Universe • Carry That Weight • Dear Prudence • Good Day Sunshine • Here Comes the Sun • If I Fell • Love Me Do • Michelle • Ob-La-Di, Ob-La-Da • Revolution • Something • Ticket to Ride • We Can Work It Out • and many more.
00703065 . . . . $19.99

BEST SONGS EVER

70 songs: All I Ask of You • Bewitched • Edelweiss • Just the Way You Are • Let It Be • Memory • Moon River • Over the Rainbow • Someone to Watch over Me • Unchained Melody • You Are the Sunshine of My Life • You Raise Me Up • and more.
00117050 . . . . $16.99

CHILDREN'S SONGS

80 classics: Alphabet Song • "C" Is for Cookie • Do-Re-Mi • I'm Popeye the Sailor Man • Mickey Mouse March • Oh! Susanna • Polly Wolly Doodle • Puff the Magic Dragon • The Rainbow Connection • Sing • Three Little Fishies (Itty Bitty Poo) • and many more.
00702473 . . . . $14.99

CHRISTMAS CAROLS

75 favorites: Away in a Manger • Coventry Carol • The First Noel • Good King Wenceslas • Hark! the Herald Angels Sing • I Saw Three Ships • Joy to the World • O Little Town of Bethlehem • Still, Still, Still • Up on the Housetop • What Child Is This? • and more.
00702474 . . . . $14.99

CHRISTMAS SONGS

55 Christmas classics: Do They Know It's Christmas? • Frosty the Snow Man • Happy Xmas (War Is Over) • Jingle-Bell Rock • Little Saint Nick • The Most Wonderful Time of the Year • White Christmas • and more.
00101776 . . . . $14.99

ISLAND SONGS

60 beach party tunes: Blue Hawaii • Day-O (The Banana Boat Song) • Don't Worry, Be Happy • Island Girl • Kokomo • Lovely Hula Girl • Mele Kalikimaka • Red, Red Wine • Surfer Girl • Tiny Bubbles • Ukulele Lady • and many more.
00702471 . . . . $16.99

150 OF THE MOST BEAUTIFUL SONGS EVER

150 melodies: Always • Bewitched • Candle in the Wind • Endless Love • In the Still of the Night • Just the Way You Are • Memory • The Nearness of You • People • The Rainbow Connection • Smile • Unchained Melody • What a Wonderful World • Yesterday • and more.
00117051 . . . . $24.99

PETER, PAUL & MARY

Over 40 songs: And When I Die • Blowin' in the Wind • Goodnight, Irene • If I Had a Hammer (The Hammer Song) • Leaving on a Jet Plane • Puff the Magic Dragon • This Land Is Your Land • We Shall Overcome • Where Have All the Flowers Gone? • and more.
00121822 . . . . $12.99

THREE CHORD SONGS

60 songs: Bad Case of Loving You • Bang a Gong (Get It On) • Blue Suede Shoes • Cecilia • Get Back • Hound Dog • Kiss • Me and Bobby McGee • Not Fade Away • Rock This Town • Sweet Home Chicago • Twist and Shout • You Are My Sunshine • and more.
00702483 . . . . $14.99

TOP HITS

31 hits: The A Team • Born This Way • Forget You • Ho Hey • Jar of Hearts • Little Talks • Need You Now • Rolling in the Deep • Teenage Dream • Titanium • We Are Never Ever Getting Back Together • and more.
00115929 . . . . $14.99

Prices, contents, and availability subject to change without notice.

7777 W. BLUEMOUND RD. P.O. BOX 13819 MILWAUKEE, WI 53213

www.halleonard.com

0814